SandCastle 3

Long Vowels

Eē

Mary Elizabeth Salzmann

ABDO
Publishing Company

Published by SandCastle™, an imprint of ABDO Publishing Company, 4940 Viking Drive, Edina, Minnesota 55435.

Printed in the United States.

Cover and Interior Photo credits: Comstock, Digital Stock, Digital Vision, Eyewire Images, Debbie Hart, Photodisc, Rubberball Productions

Library of Congress Cataloging-in-Publication Data

Salzmann, Mary Elizabeth, 1968-
   Ee / Mary Elizabeth Salzmann.
     p. cm. -- (Long vowels)
   Includes index.
   ISBN 1-57765-414-5
    1. Readers (Primary) [1. English language--Phonetics.] I. Title.

PE1119 .S23422 2000
428.1--dc21

00-033208

The SandCastle concept, content, and reading method have been reviewed and approved by a national advisory board including literacy specialists, librarians, elementary school teachers, early childhood education professionals, and parents.

Let Us Know

After reading the book, SandCastle would like you to tell us your stories about reading. What is your favorite page? Was there something hard that you needed help with? Share the ups and downs of learning to read. We want to hear from you! To get posted on the Abdo Publishing Company Web site, send us email at:

sandcastle@abdopub.com

Revised Edition 2002

About SandCastle™
Nonfiction books for the beginning reader

- Basic concepts of phonics are incorporated with integrated language methods of reading instruction. Most words are short, and phrases, letter sounds, and word sounds are repeated.

- Readability is determined by the number of words in each sentence, the number of characters in each word, and word lists based on curriculum frameworks.

- Full-color photography reinforces word meanings and concepts.

- "Words I Can Read" list at the end of each book teaches basic elements of grammar, helps the reader recognize the words in the text, and builds vocabulary.

- Reading levels are indicated by the number of flags on the castle.

Look for more SandCastle books in these three reading levels:

Level 1 (one flag)	**Level 2** (two flags)	**Level 3** (three flags)

Grades Pre-K to K 5 or fewer words per page	**Grades K to 1** 5 to 10 words per page	**Grades 1 to 2** 10 to 15 words per page

Here are some ways we have fun.

Shall we begin?

Eden tells Lena a secret.

She believes Lena will not repeat it.

Edie and Reba compete in a relay race at the picnic.

Eli and his dad prepare the newspapers to be recycled.

Ely pretends to be a superhero.

He defeats the bad guys.

Elie is taking karate lessons.

Karate is good for self-defense.

15

Enos helps Teresa reply to e-mail from her best friend.

We play hide-and-seek during recess.

Emil hides behind a tree.

Eve eats a delicious meal before school.

What is she eating?

(cereal)

Words I Can Read

Nouns

A noun is a person, place, or thing

cereal (SIHR-ee-uhl) p. 21

dad (DAD) p. 11

e-mail (EE-mayl) p. 17

friend (FREND) p. 17

fun (FUHN) p. 5

guys (GIZE) p. 13

hide-and-seek (hide-and-SEEK) p. 19

karate (kah-RAH-tee) p. 15

lessons (LESS-uhnz) p. 15

meal (MEEL) p. 21

newspapers (NOOZ-pay-purz) p. 11

picnic (PIK-nik) p. 9

recess (REE-sess) p. 19

relay race (REE-lay rayss) p. 9

school (SKOOL) p. 21

secret (SEE-krit) p. 7

self-defense (self-di-FENSS) p. 15

superhero (SOO-pur-hihr-oh) p. 13

tree (TREE) p. 19

ways (WAYZ) p. 5

Proper Nouns

A proper noun is the name of a person, place, or thing

Eden (EE-duhn) p. 7

Edie (EE-dee) p. 9

Eli (EE-lye) p. 11

Elie (EE-lee) p. 15

Ely (EE-lye) p. 13

Emil (EE-mil) p. 19

Enos (EE-nuhss) p. 17

Eve (EEV) p. 21

Lena (LEE-nuh) p. 7

Reba (REE-buh) p. 9

Teresa (tur-EESS-uh) p. 17

Pronouns

A pronoun is a word that replaces a noun

he (HEE) p. 13

it (IT) p. 7

she (SHEE) pp. 7, 21

we (WEE) pp. 5, 19

what (WUHT) p. 21

Verbs
A verb is an action or being word

are (AR) p. 5
be (BEE) pp. 11, 13
begin (bee-GIN) p. 5
believes (bee-LEEVZ) p. 7
compete (kuhm-PEET) p. 9
defeats (dee-FEETSS) p. 13
eating (EET-ing) p. 21

eats (EETSS) p. 21
have (HAV) p. 5
helps (HELPSS) p. 17
hides (HIDEZ) p. 19
is (IZ) pp. 15, 21
play (PLAY) p. 19
prepare (pree-PAIR) p. 11
pretends (pree-TENDZ) p. 13

recycled (ree-SYE-kuhld) p. 11
repeat (ree-PEET) p. 7
reply (ree-PLYE) p. 17
shall (SHAL) p. 5
taking (TAYK-ing) p. 15
tells (TELZ) p. 7
will (WIL) p. 7

Adjectives
An adjective describes something

bad (BAD) p. 13
best (BEST) p. 17
delicious (di-LISH-uhss) p. 21

good (GUD) p. 15
her (HUR) p. 17
his (HIZ) p. 11

karate (kah-RAH-tee) p. 15
some (SUHM) p. 5

Adverbs
An adverb tells how, when, or where something happens

here (HIHR) p. 5

not (NOT) p. 7

23

Glossary

cereal – a breakfast food usually made from grain and eaten with milk.

e-mail – messages that are sent using computers and the Internet.

karate – a form of self-defense that uses controlled kicks and punches.

relay race – a team race in which members take turns carrying something (usually a baton).

More Ēē Words

because	idea	report
belong	legal	scene
decide	maybe	these
enough	me	zebra
even	meow	zero

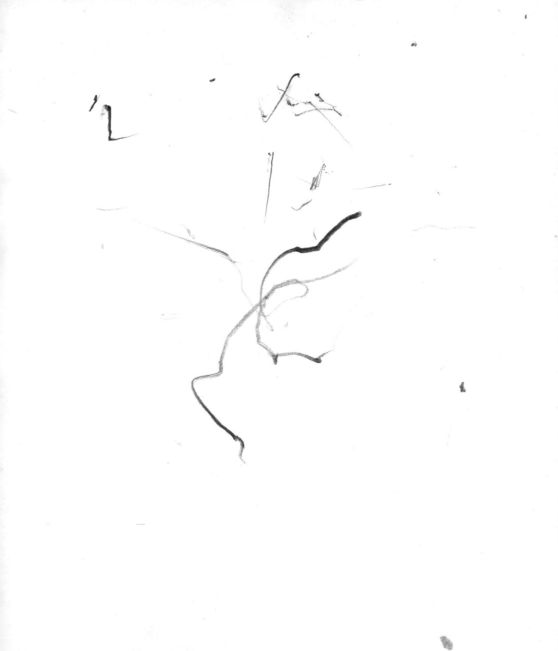